WHAT PEOPLE ARE SAYING ABOUT *RISK IT!*...

"Reva Nelson has provided a strategy for stepping beyond limitations. Caution: reading this book could be hazardous to your status quo."

— Harold Taylor,
Consultant and Author

"I enjoyed *Risk it!*. By the time I finished it, I was rarin' to go!"

— June Rogers,
Journalist

"If you're on a treadmill, you're probably taking no risks. Here's a book to help you take your first liberating steps to freedom."

— David Schatzky,
*Broadcaster and Executive
Director,
The Children's Broadcast
Institute*

"Invaluable help for employees and companies to take risks and find ways to meet the challenges of the global marketplace."

— Carol Barby, *CMP,
Manager, Meetings
and Conferences
The Society of Management
Accountants of Ontario*

"I read **Risk it!** the first time out of curiosity. I read it a second time for me."

— Vicki Dickson,
Sales Training Manager
Boehringer Ingelheim
(Canada) Ltd.

"I recommend this guide heartily to anyone—manager, supervisor, professional or person-on-the-street—who wishes to take more risks but cannot. **Risk it!** is a valuable tool to enrich lives and improve performance."

— Dr. Paul Preston,
Professor of Management
University of Texas

RISK *it !*

HOW TO OVERCOME FEAR AND MAKE SMART CHANGES

by
Reva Nelson

Published by Words.Worth Professional Communications, Toronto, Ontario, Canada.

Canadian Cataloguing in Publication Data

Nelson, Reva, 1948-
    Risk it! : how to overcome fear and make smart changes

Includes bibliographical references.
ISBN 0-9695410-0-7

1. Risk-taking (Psychology). 2. Fear. 3. Decision-making
4. Self-help techniques. I. Title.

BF637.R57N45 1991   158'.1   C91-095247-7

The Production Team

Cover design: Kristine Ramezani
Typesetting: Hope Thompson
Illustrations: Brian Fray
Photo: Glamour Shots
Printing: Webcom

ACKNOWLEDGEMENTS

Maria Stebelski and Don Malpass, formerly of the Human Resources Secretariat, Government of Ontario, who first opened the door for me to facilitate my "Risk-taking" workshops in 1985, and Chris Crapper of Ontario Hydro who asked for a "Risk-taker's Guide".

The clients who continue to hire my company and refer me to others.

My colleagues at the National Speakers Association, Ontario chapter, and The Mastermind, Third Line, Markovitz and Wishcraft groups.

My writer friends who offered encouragement and helped edit this guidebook: June Rogers, Jane Watson and Marcia Kaye.

All those who offered me support, laughter and honest feedback in my own passage.

My son Jonathan, who lights my way with a pure heart and a bright spirit.

PROFILES

Of the fifteen risk-takers profiled in this guide, some are the famous recipients of several awards, and some are unknown. I became re-energized about this project by talking with them. I thank them all for their time and candor. They touched my heart.

DEDICATION

In loving memory of my sister-in-law,
Evelyn Roden Nelson, an analytical mathematician
who believed in me even when she disagreed,
and of my friend Judith Defren, a writer
who hated exclamation marks!

TABLE OF CONTENTS

Introduction *1*

Risk-taking Objectives *3*

Why Take Risks: Personal *5*

    PROFILE: Sharon Wood *9*

Why Take Risks: Corporate *11*

Risk-taking: Definition *15*

    PROFILE: Dave Broadfoot *17*

OBJECTIVE 1
*To Become Aware of Personal and Corporate
Attitudes Toward Risk-taking* *19*

    PROFILE: Cheryl Wagner *27*

    PROFILE: Jeff MacInnis *35*

    PROFILE: Ed Mirvish *37*

OBJECTIVE 2
To Identify the Factors which Enable Risk-taking *39*

    PROFILE: Paul Howard *43*

    PROFILE: Carl Hiebert *47*

OBJECTIVE 3
To Identify the Factors which Inhibit Risk-taking. *49*

    PROFILE: Jonathan Nelson *55*

OBJECTIVE 4
*To Understand the Risk Cycle and When to Use It
in order to Take Risks Wisely* *57*

    PROFILE: Bonnie Bickel *63*

    PROFILE: John Kim Bell *75*

    PROFILE: Marg Gleeson *77*

    PROFILE: Bonney King *79*

OBJECTIVE 5
*To Comprehend the Relationship of Intuition,
Creativity and Risk-taking to Innovation* *81*

    PROFILE: John Easton *87*

OBJECTIVE 6
*To Learn How You and Your Company
can be Mutually Supportive in order to
Take the Risks Necessary to Innovate* *89*

    PROFILE: Fred Ryan *95*

    PROFILE: June Callwood *105*

Suggested Reading

INTRODUCTION

Risk-taking is a topic that has fascinated me for more than fifteen years. Why? Because I'm basically a chicken. In fact, I was raised on chicken soup and guilt! I do, however, have a tremendous curiosity and "joie de vivre". I'm idealistic by nature. So I have driven myself to take risks in spite of my fears. I believe my life has been fuller, richer, more interesting and more exciting because of the risks I've taken. This conviction has made me want to help others take risks.

I find it disturbing when people hold themselves back from something they'd like to accomplish because of the fear of risk-taking. They would rather minimize joy to maximize safety. I also believe that when we are not excited about life, we are not living as fully and as "healthfully" as we might. People start to complain, get sick, be unmotivated and uninterested in others, if they don't like themselves or their lives much. In company terms, this malaise results in poor morale, unhappy employees, increased illness and lost time.

There are so many changes happening so quickly in our society that we need to become more innovative on both personal and corporate levels. Risk-taking is a very important component of innovation, along with intuition and creativity. If corporations want to become more innovative, they must learn how to encourage and support risk-taking. It costs time and energy not to risk.

We need to take risks to challenge and enjoy life. Risk-taking is essential for growth, change and the realization of our human and professional potential.

It is my intention to share my enthusiasm for risk-taking with you. It's too easy to read about ideas but not work with them. I invite you to interact with this guide, pencil in hand.

Good luck!

Reva Nelson,
Toronto, 1991

RISK-TAKING OBJECTIVES

1. To become aware of personal and corporate attitudes toward risk-taking.

2. To identify the factors which encourage risk-taking.

3. To identify the factors which inhibit risk-taking.

4. To understand the "risk-cycle" and how to use it to take risks wisely.

5. To comprehend the relationship of intuition, creativity and risk-taking to innovation.

6. To learn how you and your company can be mutually supportive in taking the risks that are necessary for innovation.

4 ◆ RISK *it!*

WHY TAKE RISKS: PERSONAL

"SHIPS ARE SAFE IN THE HARBOUR, BUT IT'S NOT WHAT THEY WERE BUILT FOR."

We need to take risks to have lives that are filled with vitality and meaning.

Babies are terrific risk-takers. They have tremendous curiosity and drive. They take enormous chances several times each day and face a multitude of failures.

Think of a baby trying to walk. She falls down, over and over again. She bumps her head, but knows no fear. She's determined.

Each effort is not seen as a failure, but as an attempt. We expect babies to risk, fail, risk again and then keep on trying until they get it right. If we had any idea how many times we'd fail when we were learning how to walk, we'd all still be in our cribs.

Thomas Edison said "I failed my way to success." He said that each failure was an attempt that told him something that he needed to know in order to eventually succeed.

Risk-taking is scary for everyone—less so for some, more so for others. No one likes to face the possibility of failure, ridicule, making mistakes or looking foolish.

We learn to play it safe, often at a high cost to ourselves and our companies. We use up energy by not risking.

We're not encouraged to listen to our own sense of direction, our inner voice, our intuition. In fact, we tend to ignore it, because listening can mean taking risks.

It's our inner voice that inspires us to take risks, and the voice of fear that we allow to stop us.

It's our inner voice that says:	Our non-risking voice says:
"Maybe I should try for that position."	*"I'm not good enough."*
"I think I'm right about this proposal. I'll have to talk to my boss again."	*"No sense stirring things up."*
"We don't have enough support staff to do this amount of work."	*"I'd better not say anything" or I'll get fired."*
"This relationship is in serious trouble."	*"If I even begin to look at this, it will lead to our separation."*
"I'd really like to spend my next vacation doing something different—maybe going to the Arctic or Africa."	*"I don't have (and won't ever get) the money."*
"I really should go back to University and get my degree (or begin the next one.)"	*"I'll probably fail."*

If we choose to, we can stay safe, like the ship in the harbour. By doing so, we sacrifice adventure, learning about ourselves, and growth. In fact, we go against our life force (wellness) and give our death force (illness) a full berth.

Why do we protect ourselves so much? Is it so important to be able to say, "Phew, I made it to death safely?" We have a choice of rusting out from inertia or wearing out from use. It is our responsibility to live our lives fully.

To do so, we must take risks.

PROFILE: SHARON WOOD

In 1986, Sharon Wood became the first North American woman to reach the top of Mount Everest. She is 34, a climbing instructor, mountain guide, wife, mother, public speaker and workshop facilitator.

THE RISK I never considered myself to be confident; I had to work hard at it. I left home at age 16. I was attracted to climbing and the positive attitude of those trying it. With encouragement, I began to realize I was as strong as anyone else. My big risk was even to apply to get on the 1986 Mount Everest climbing team.

THE FEAR I had a greater fear of not measuring up, of losing face, than I ever did of falling. In climbing difficulties, I would either freeze, then tell myself to get out of it, or, the adrenaline would kick in, because I had to perform.

THE RESULT I did it! It was a team effort of thirteen climbers plus two support people; my struggle was the inner one. I gained confidence and reached my personal best by pushing myself.

"PEOPLE DON'T CONQUER MOUNTAINS, THEY CONQUER THE INNER MOUNTAIN OF THEIR OWN FEARS."

WHY TAKE RISKS: CORPORATE

> *"THE REAL ORGANIZATION YOU ARE WORKING FOR*
> *'OUT THERE' AND THE ONE 'IN HERE' ARE NOT TWO*
> *SEPARATE THINGS. THEY GROW TOWARDS EXCELLENCE*
> *TOGETHER."*
>
> Richard Pasquale,
> *Zen and the Art of Management*

A corporation can't expect its people to take risks until each person examines risk-taking on a personal level first. It takes self-knowledge and self-confidence to take risks within a corporation.

Most people tell me that there is not the encouragement, the environment or the corporate culture in which to risk. Employees say, "I'm not putting my neck on the line." or "The message around here is don't rock the boat," "I can't make a difference. I'm too low on the totem pole." or "I'm here to get my boss re-elected. That's it."

I can't blame them. In that environment, I'm not sure I'd want to speak up either. If I did, I'd have to have a strong sense of self, of the importance of what I had to say, and the feeling that I absolutely *had* to take the risk, or leave. My own integrity would have to be on the line.

I've actually been in that situation. As a consultant at a University, I did speak up for a secretary who was so overworked, she was close to either a nervous breakdown, or quitting. I was so surprised that my manager planned to do nothing and that he had no contingency funds in the budget for such emergencies, that I said so. He told me never to criticize him at a meeting again. I was on contract, and it was not renewed.

Although I was in shock at the time, I eventually received a more lucrative contract and a better position.

Later, I started my own business. The secretary received assistance. I was young then and somewhat naïve about office politics. However, it ended well. Was it a difficult time to go through? Most definitely. But I knew I'd done the right thing and that I could live with myself. I never would have been happy working with that manager. I still believe honesty pays off in the long run. Your integrity will be recognized eventually. Most importantly, *you* know the risk taken and the difference you made.

An organization has to value its people. The individuals within the corporation will become even more important as we strive to anticipate and respond to the changes in our future. As Alvin Toffler, author of *The Third Wave*, and John Naisbitt, *Megatrends*, say, we are changing from a hierarchy to a network of individuals. It is the creative, self-actualized and motivated individual who will be able to lead the way in today's corporation and tomorrow's economy. The organization must choose to take its leadership from the individuals within in order to achieve a shared vision.

We need to be innovative in order to find new methods. We need strategies to save the environment, promote energy efficiency, develop new products, find better ways of working with people, provide quality customer service and raise the quality of each individual's working life.

All innovation begins with one person, with an idea, who will take the risks to put the idea forward and find the team to develop it.

The corporation has to provide the environment for that individual to feel safe to take the risk. Mistakes and failure need to be understood and accepted as part of the process toward the vision. Resources such as time, money and personnel have to be provided. A reward system must be in place.

There must be initiative on the part of the individual, support on the part of the corporation and trust between the two.

Do you have that now?

Before we look at *Objective #1: Personal and Corporate Attitudes Toward Risk-Taking,* let's be sure we have a good definition of risk-taking.

RISK-TAKING: DEFINITION

The exercise of reaching consensus on the definition of risk *is* a risk for the participants of my seminars because everyone has his own idea of which words are critical for the definition. Let's go through the process together:

Risk is most often defined as a negative factor, a hazard, something to be controlled, managed or eliminated.

The Oxford Dictionary definition is: To risk is to hazard, to endanger, to expose to the chance of injury or loss.

Most magazines and "free trial" offers come with a "no risk" guarantee. Banks tend to be "risk aversive"; you can get the loan once you can prove you're in good financial shape and don't really need the money!

I, of course, want to change the concept of risk from a negative to a positive one.

If you think of risk-taking as a positive action to accomplish a particular goal, there are then other words that take on more importance in the definition. Listed on the next page are words that can be put together to create a new, more exciting definition.

Exercise:
Working toward a definition

1. Circle the words that you find particularly meaning-
    ful for a definition of Risk-Taking:

VISION	SUCCESS	COMMITMENT
EXCEED	FAILURE	LOSS
PERCEPTION	STRIVE	GOALS
FEAR	DETERMINATION	DECISION
LIMITATIONS	DRIVE	EXCELLENCE
ACTION	HAZARD	POSSIBLE
BELIEF	CHANCE	DREAM
POSITIVE	NEGATIVE	

2. Using some of the words you circled, try your hand
    at writing a definition of Risk-Taking:

    _____

    _____

    _____

    _____

    _____

    _____

    _____

3. The act of finding a definition of risk-taking that is
    the right one for you is a worthwhile process. It
    develops your ability to understand and integrate
    the different factors involved in taking risks in your
    life. Certain factors of the definition are critical to
    this core understanding.

PROFILE: DAVE BROADFOOT

Dave Broadfoot has spent nearly 40 years as a professional comedy writer and performer.

A multi-award winner, he has delighted audiences of the CBC radio show, "The Royal Canadian Air Farce" for fifteen years and is in his third year of touring in "Dave Broadfoot's Comedy Crusade".

THE RISK At the age of 20, I wanted to join amateur theatre, but it took me a whole year to get up the courage to apply. While acting in my first comedy, I heard the laughter and got hooked. My big risk was to quit my saleman's job in Vancouver to plunge into professional theatre, which I did at age 25.

THE FEAR I never had much fear of the audience. My fear was that I wouldn't be able to make the monthly mortgage payments on the house I had bought for my parents to help them out of the "rent, move, rent" cycle. I went into debt a few times and had to have my brother in Montreal co-sign some loans.

THE RESULT I moved to Toronto in 1952, the day TV started. Two months later I was on it. I was determined to succeed and I did, because I have been able to spend a lifetime doing something I love.

I've never been a giant international star. But I had a young woman tell me that shortly before her husband died, he had seen me perform and laughed so hard that he forgot about his pain. She thanked me for the joy that I gave him that evening. This type of accolade is very meaningful to me.

"SOME PEOPLE SPEND A LIFETIME FEELING TRAPPED IN WORK THEY HATE. IF THAT'S YOUR LIFE, WHAT ARE YOU GIVING UP BY TAKING A RISK?"

Factors:

A. A conscious *decision* to act, to move on the idea.

B. There are *no guarantees* in risk-taking. We risk when we *think* we will succeed, but we don't *know* the outcome.

C. *Vision* - we must take risks *for* something, a desired outcome or goal.

Here are three definitions of risk-taking. Circle the one you like best. Make any changes necessary to improve your definition.

Risk-taking Definitions:

1. To move into action to achieve a desired outcome in spite of possible loss and no guarantee of success.

2. To take action for a goal after weighing the options and deciding there is a greater chance of a positive outcome than a negative one.

3. To decide to go beyond your usual limitations to achieve a vision when you believe success is more likely than failure.

OBJECTIVE 1

TO BECOME AWARE OF PERSONAL AND CORPORATE ATTITUDES TOWARD RISK-TAKING

A. Personal Attitudes Toward Risk-Taking
To assess your attitudes, please answer the following questions as spontaneously as possible:

	Yes	No
1. I think that I am a risk-taker.		
2. I find it difficult to take risks.		
3. I tend to do what "the norm" is.		
4. I always try to please others.		
5. My intuition plays an important role in my choice of jobs.		
6. I think that I'm creative.		
7. I like to try different kinds of restaurants and foods.		
8. I think that I "follow the beat of a different drummer".		
9. I got a job right after school and have worked steadily ever since.		
10. My friends are from different backgrounds and fields of interest.		
11. I like to be spontaneous.		

	Yes	No
12. I would never think of travelling around the world.		
13. I tend to like to do the same activities most weekends.		
14. Job security is very high on my list of priorities.		
15. My fantasy life bears no resemblance to my real life.		
16. I have no fantasy life!		
17. I usually have the same opinions about politics, work and family life as most of the people I know.		
18. I have never taken a day off work when I was not sick in order to enjoy the day.		

Personal Attitudes: Answers

This is not a scientific questionnaire. In a sense, there are not even any "right" or "wrong" answers. The questions only serve to assist you in becoming aware of some of your attitudes.

Q1: *I think that I am a risk-taker.*

A1: If you answered "yes" then you probably are a risk-taker. Risk-taking is personal, so whatever you perceive to be a risk for you, is one. For example, I have a fear of falling, so skiing, skating and mountain climbing are all very risky for me.

If you answered "no" then you are probably thinking of a risk you wish you had taken but did not take. Start to think of risks you did take.

Q2: *I find it difficult to take risks.*

A2: EVERYONE finds it difficult to take risks—that's why we perceive it as a risk! Fear is as much a part of risk-taking as chicken is of chicken soup!

Q3: *I tend to do what "the norm" is.*

A3:. Most risk-takers are quite independent and do not follow the crowd.

Q4: *I always try to please others.*

A4: If you answered, "Yes," then it will be harder for you to risk. When you take a risk, it's very difficult to please others as well. Sometimes you have to take that chance. However, honesty of intentions and talking about what you want to do, and why, makes it easier to take the risk.

Q5: *My intuition plays an important role in my choice of jobs.*

A5: Risk-taking involves using your intuition and not just taking whatever comes along. A sense of "what feels right" is necessary.

Q6: *I think that I'm creative.*

A6: There are so many different ways to be creative in finding new solutions to problems and generating options. If you don't think you are very creative, know that creativity is something that we all have, which can be released. Do something different. Go walk in a different neighborhood. See a foreign film. Read a humour book. Break up your normal pattern. A change in routine can stimulate the creative process.

Q7: *I like to try different kinds of restaurants and foods.*

A7: Terrific! Be open to new experiences. It helps you be more creative and take more risks.

Q8: *I think that I "follow the beat of a different drummer".*

A8: If you answered "yes" to this one, then you probably are already a risk-taker. If "no" was your answer, try to get a sense of your own thoughts, feelings and "inner voice" about issues. It can be difficult to be different from the crowd, but it's a necessary part of risk-taking.

Q9: *I got a job right after school and have worked steadily ever since.*

A9: Good for you—it's the way most of us were raised. However, you may have limited some of your life experiences which then can limit your perceptions of the importance of issues when they may not be so life-important! Broadening your experiential base helps you generate options and see more solutions to problems. Maybe you can plan a vacation to an exotic place!

Q10: *My friends are from different backgrounds and fields of interest.*

A10: Again, broadening your base of friends enables you to have many more perceptions, thoughts and ideas and can help in your risk-taking ability.

Q11: *I like to be spontaneous.*

A11: Spontaneity helps you break the pattern and have some fun. The most creative people are child-like and playful. (This is different than childish and immature.) Do something spontaneous and different tonight!

Q12: *I would never think of travelling around the world.*

A12: I'm not saying *do* it—just think about it! Where *could* you travel to?

Q13: *I tend to like to do the same activities most weekends.*

A13: We are such creatures of habit. Again, doing something quite different, whether it's seeing your first ballet or baseball game, can "up" your risk potential.

Q14: *Job security is very high on my list of priorities.*

A14: Good! You help the economy be more secure. However, all kinds of variations are possible. For example, if you never got your degree, you can at least *ask* about working part time or having a leave of absence for educational purposes—if it's important to you. Also, to risk within a corporation you might have to be willing to put your job on the line.

Q15: *My fantasy life bears no resemblance to my real life.*

A15: Of course, it depends what you mean by this. However, all risk should start from some vision of what you would like to see happen. So if you fantasize about having your own business or travelling in Mexico, decide if you really want that to happen. Is it a vision worth risking for?

Q16: *I have no fantasy life!*

A16: Boring! Get one. Take the time to dream. Research different careers. Read travel brochures.

Q17: I usually have the same opinions about politics, work and family life as most of the people I know.

A17: If "yes", you either have a very narrow group of friends or you have no opinions. Differences are normal and necessary. (You can disagree with that statement, of course.)

Q18: I have never taken a day off work when I was not sick in order to enjoy the day.

A18: I won't tell. Often one mental health day can avert ten sick days. What's life for? Enjoy yourself. You can choose to be healthy and not sick. Risk-takers need to be in good health.

PROFILE: CHERYL WAGNER

At age 24, Cheryl formed the Grindstone Island Co-op Company to run programs on international peace. She entered medical school at age 29, then worked in Northwestern native communities as a "fly-in" Doctor. In 1986 she joined a Doctor's practice in Toronto that included many AIDS patients. When she became pregnant, she continued working.

THE RISK I didn't perceive working with AIDS patients as very risky. It felt a lot safer than flying through snowstorms to remote communities. At least I'd be on the ground.

THE FEAR What I did not anticipate was the social reaction of my having these clients. One group of doctors that courted me to join them, unsuccessfully, basically said they wanted me but not my patients.

I had minimal fear for my baby because my information was based on knowledge, not supposition or prejudice.

THE RESULT Physicians have traditionally been exposed to the diseases of their patients. Anything that I experience is so minimal compared to what seriously ill people experience every day.

It was reassuring for my clients to see life in the face of so much death, and for the other thirty per cent of my practise who do not have AIDS to see me carry on with confidence about our mutual health safety.

I did not put my baby at risk, nor would I. She is perfectly healthy. I hope that by the time she grows up, society will be free of such prejudice.

"THE MORE DIFFICULT CHALLENGES USUALLY BRING THE GREATEST REWARDS."

Corporate Attitudes Toward Risk-Taking

	Yes	No
1. I tend to keep quiet at meetings even when I have some good ideas.		
2. Most people at work see me as innovative. They wonder how I get to do the projects that are challenging and interesting.		
3. If I felt stagnated in my job I would not say anything or try to introduce a new system or project.		
4. I would rather change jobs than convince my manager or supervisor of my worth and talent.		
5. I often volunteer to introduce and thank speakers in my organization.		
6. There is a lot of trust and support for new ideas in my organization.		
7. If I proposed a good idea and was able to show it could be cost effective, chances are I'd get the time and money to work on it.		
8. I am in a senior position. I take a lot of risks. My staff, however, does not.		
9. There is too much bureaucracy and paper-work here to facilitate any change.		
10. We have no money for any risks to be taken around here.		

Corporate Attitude: Comments

Q1: *I tend to keep quiet at meetings even when I have some good ideas.*

A1   Anyone who wants to take risks within a corporation has to meet the corporation at least half-way. It's imperative to speak up at meetings and put new ideas forward. Nothing can happen otherwise. However, if the meeting is not run properly and the environment is not a safe one for putting ideas forward without being ridiculed and met with negativity—then I don't blame you! Try forming an alliance with one or two like-minded people first.

Q2: *Most people at work see me as innovative. They wonder how I get to do the projects that are challenging and interesting.*

A2   Risk-takers are innovative. They feel that they can make a difference. The way to get to do interesting projects is to believe in yourself and propose them.

Q3 *If I felt stagnated in my job, I would not say anything or try to introduce a new system or project.*

A3   Nothing will change without some degree of personal risk. Most people complain, moan and groan about their dead-end jobs. It's true that many jobs *are* dead-end which is extremely frustrating. But there comes a point in time when a serious look at yourself *and* the job are necessary.

Ask yourself:
1) Is this the only job I can get with these qualifications?
2) If yes, can I get more qualified?
3) Is there something I can do that can make this job more interesting?

4)   Who can I talk to about this problem?

Many people complain but will not take any action toward change. It's imperative to either accept things as they are, or take the risks to change the situation or your own attitudes, qualifications or area of abilities.

Q4:   I would rather change jobs than convince my manager or supervisor of my worth and talent.

A4   It's very hard to speak up for what you want to see happen, especially in a negative environment. You simply have to believe in yourself and your worth. If the environment is truly unsupportive and you've really made the effort, then the best thing to do might be to look elsewhere within the corporation. Who are the managers who support risk-taking? Where is innovation taking place? Try to get on a supportive team.

Q5:   I often volunteer to introduce and thank speakers in my organization.

A5   Great! One of the biggest risks for many people is public speaking. If you can volunteer for it, it will increase your confidence and raise your potential for risk-taking.

Q6:   There is a lot of trust and support for new ideas in my organization.

A6   Terrific if it's true. Unfortunately it often isn't. Get to know who the supportive managers are. Bring in training programs or videos to support change, risk and innovation. Attitudes take a long time to form and a longer time to change!

Q7: *If I proposed a good idea and was able to show it could be cost effective, chances are I'd get the time and money to work on it.*

A7 Good organizations will make available time, money and personnel to support risk-taking and innovative ideas. Does yours?

Q8: *I am in a senior position. I take a lot of risks. My staff, however, does not.*

A8 As a senior administrator, one has to think of "risking downward". What support systems are in place to encourage your people to take risks? Do you provide training in creativity, risk and innovation? Do you have a clear forum for new ideas?

Q9: *There is too much bureaucracy and paperwork here to facilitate any change.*

A9 People can't innovate when there are too many levels to go through. Take a cold hard look at procedures. What doesn't need to have ten forms and six approvals?

Q10: *We have no money for any risks to be taken around here.*

A10 Money has a magical way of appearing once senior levels approve the project. Involve many levels in your team. Generate enthusiasm. Have a clear plan. Be convincing. Show ways to cut costs in other areas. Have a clear vision.

Here's another way to assess the corporate attitude toward risk-taking. Check the response that you would be most likely to hear in your organization for each of the following statements:

1. **New Idea**
   Response:
   a) That's terrific. I think that's a great idea.
      Let's try it. ☐
   b) That will never work. There's no ☐
      i) time
      ii) money
      iii) personnel
      iv) whatever
   c) We've tried that before. It didn't work. ☐

2. **Change**
   Response:
   a) No changes are on the horizon right now. ☐
   b) There's gonna be a lotta changes around
      here and they're happenin' fast so get ready. ☐
   c) We anticipate a few changes but don't panic. ☐
      The changes will be slow and you'll all have
      a chance to be involved. We need your input.

3. **Training**
   Response:
   a) Training is a waste of time. The budget's cut. ☐
   b) This course fits the needs analysis. I want
      you to take it. Finish your work on the
      weekend. ☐
   c) You perceive this course to be of value?
      I'm sure we can fit it into the budget
      —go ahead. ☐

4. Mistakes

Response:

a) One mistake and you're fired. ❑

b) I'm not thrilled about this mistake but I'm glad you went ahead and took the risk. I support your effort here. Can you do two things now? Fix it, or show me how you'll avoid this next time. Also, I want to know what it cost us and methods to recover the money. What else do you propose? ❑

c) Well, I know we said we allow mistakes, but this one just cost accounting $47.29. Wasn't it avoidable? ❑

5. Innovation

Response:

a) No need to innovate here. Everything works just fine. ❑

b) Let's innovate. I want 10 ways to do things differently on my desk by 8:00 a.m. tomorrow.
Why? I don't know. It's the new "in" thing. ❑

c) We simply can't be responsive to change in a reactive, knee-jerk manner. Let's look for opportunities and take some risks. Why don't we schedule three brain-storming sessions and see what ideas we generate? I'll free up some time for you to get out of the office for a day as well. ❑

Obviously answers a,c,c,b and c are the ones that promote proactive thinking and opportunities. Do they sound like a fairy tale? It doesn't need to be some unattainable castle in the clouds.

What are your corporation's attitudes toward: risk, change, mistakes and innovation?

Try "tracking" what you hear and see around the office.

At least you'll know what you're dealing with when it's time to take some risks. If you're changing companies, these questions can help you assess the new organization. Is their corporate culture one that you want to work in?

PROFILE: JEFF MACINNIS

At age 28, Jeff is an explorer and corporate speaker. He completed the historic first sail through the Northwest Passage of the Arctic on an eighteen foot catamaran during the summers of 1986 to 1988.

THE RISK There have been three main risks. I represented Canada in the world cup downhill ski race in 1982-1983, I speak to large corporate audiences, and the Polar journey, which, in four hundred years of effort, had never been done before. It has claimed more lives than the attempts to climb Mt. Everest.

The voyage was a physical and mental challenge. It was a test of my Self, and I passed the test.

THE FEAR The Arctic is one of the most hostile environments on the planet. The ice shifts all the time and the freezing waters and polar bears can kill you.

THE RESULT I saw an idea that I had at age twenty-one become a reality within four years. This had a real impact on me. The voyage resulted in my book, *Polar Passage*, a speaking career, and a National Geographic story.

"WE CAN ALL DREAM, DARE AND DO. THERE ARE SO MANY OPPORTUNITIES FOR BOLD NEW DISCOVERIES."

36 ◆ RISK *it!*

Project: **Discover Your Corporation's Attitudes**

Method: "Tracking"

Tracking is a useful tool to assess current attitudes and behaviors. To do it, you "follow" and "keep track" of what people say, and how often they say and do it!

Task: Attend 3 meetings
Listen for new ideas and the responses to them. Fill in the list below.

Corporate Attitudes To: (Fill in what was actually said)	Positive eg. "Let's expand on that"	Negative eg. "That won't work"
A. A New Idea		
B. Change		
C. Training		
D. Mistakes		
E. Innovation		
F. (Other)		

PROFILE: ED MIRVISH

Ed Mirvish is the owner of "Honest Ed's", the large bargain shopping store that has become a Toronto tourist attraction. He is also the developer of Mirvish village, an area of restaurants, galleries and boutiques, the owner and refurbisher of two famous old theatres, the employer of over 1,000 people, planner of a new theatre and recipient of many awards.

THE RISK Over fifty years ago, I cashed my wife's insurance policy for $215. in order to get the $55./month rent for my first store. I had little money or formal education. Later, in 1962, I bought the Royal Alex theatre before its demolition. I didn't know about theatre; I just thought it was a bargain. Then I developed six restaurants next to it. In 1982, I bought the Old Vic in London, England. When a theatre's locked up, you know what it's costing you. Put something on stage and you can go bankrupt.

THE FEAR When I rented my first store, I was afraid I wouldn't be able to meet my obligations. Every penny was important. But if you're busy and excited about new ideas and goals, you don't have time to be afraid. Some wealthy people have overextended themselves financially. To me that's not risk-taking; it's gambling. That's much different.

THE RESULT I went from selling groceries on Dundas St., at age fifteen when my father died, to receiving honours at Buckingham Palace. Every day is a holiday for me. I'm 77 now. If I can get up in the morning and tie my shoelaces, it's a great day.

"SUCCESS CAN BE MEASURED IN DIFFERENT WAYS. IF YOU'RE FREE TO DO WHAT YOU WANT TO DO, WHEN YOU WANT TO DO IT, THAT'S SUCCESS."

As Stephen Lewis, Canada's former ambassador to the United Nations said, "Social change does not happen by Divine Intervention." Begin to think of the risks you would have to take to move your organization to become more innovative, open and accepting of risk-taking.

Taken any risks lately?

In 1974 Phillipe Petit strung a wire across the twin towers of the World Trade Centre in New York City and went for a stroll 1350 feet above the pavement. Like many risk-takers, he does not consider himself to be one. He thinks day-to-day living is riskier, and is afraid of spiders.

Risk Arenas

Before we begin to look at "RISK ENABLERS" and "RISK INHIBITORS" we need to consider the fact that there are many different types of risks. We often think of investments (FINANCIAL RISK) or job-changes (OCCUPATIONAL RISK) but there are six areas or "RISK ARENAS" to consider. Once you start to explore these, you may discover that you are more of a risk-taker than you thought!

1. *Risk Arenas*

A	**PHYSICAL**	Test yourself against yourself. Some personal growth takes place. It's not the same as "thrill-seeking". *Example:* Learning to ski, rock-climb or practice T'ai-chi
B	**EMOTIONAL**	It could be getting married, *or*, deciding to get "unmarried". *Example:* Deciding to go to a marriage counsellor. Being honest with a friend, boss or employee.
C	**OCCUPATIONAL**	Refusing the manager's position because you like what you're doing now. *Example:* You don't take the promotion because you don't want to move.
D	**FINANCIAL**	Not just investing. Deciding to take a year off could be a big financial risk. *Example:* Setting aside a special fund for education or travel.

E INTELLECTUAL   Going back to university or just taking a different sort of course.
                 Example: Sign-up for a lecture series.

F SPIRITUAL   Renouncing your religion *or* returning to it *or* investigating other topics, such as reincarnation.
                 Example: Attend a friend's place of worship.

2. *Risk-taking is very personal*
    You should always take your own risks—not someone else's. For example, if you become a lawyer to please your parents, you'll never be happy no matter how good you are.

3. *What's risky for one person is not a risk for someone else.*
    Eg. I'm not afraid to travel alone but I'm afraid to go skiing!

PROFILE: PAUL HOWARD

In July of 1983, Paul Howard, free-lance writer, author, sailor and house renovator, with his wife, Fiona McCall, who gave up her job of Communications Director at Harbourfront, in Toronto, and their two children, Peter, age 4, and Penny, age six, left land for sea. They intended to sail for a few years. Their journey took them around the world for five years and led to two books and a television documentary.

THE RISK We had a thirty-foot sailboat outfitted to withstand a full gale at sea. There's always a possibility of hurricanes and cyclones, but we studied their patterns carefully and only sailed in the safe times. Our health and safety were the biggest risks.

THE FEAR Our fears included piracy and being run down at sea by other ships. We kept a 24-hour watch, switching positions every three hours, sometimes at thirty days for a stretch.

We feared for the children's health. We were far from land and sometimes went twenty-four days at sea without seeing even another ship.

THE RESULT We were almost run over by a ship near Australia but pulled away just in time.

Peter did run a high fever. We had full medical provisions and began to administer an antibiotic, but we were 800 miles out. At 100 miles a day, that's eight days to reach shore. We didn't know if the medicine would be effective. Fortunately, Peter recovered, and both children remained healthy.

The main result is, WE DID IT! We all learned about the world and ourselves. All travel is a voyage of discovery.

"TAKING A RISK IS ALWAYS AN EXPANDING EXPERIENCE THAT ENRICHES OUR LIVES, NO MATTER WHAT THE TURN OUT."

Risk Enablers

1. Think of 3 risks you have taken that you are glad you took.
2. Place the 3 risks into the risk arenas on the chart below.

Risk Arenas	Risks Taken	Age at the time
Physical		
Emotional		
Occupational		
Financial		
Intellectual		
Spiritual		

What "risk arenas" do most of your risks fall into?

_____

_____

Are you now able to perceive yourself as a "risk-taker"?

_____

_____

Risk Enablers

What enabled you to take these risks you listed?
List at least 5 *"Risk Enablers"*

1.

2.

3.

4.

5.

Some of the "risk enablers" identified by seminar participants are listed below:
• confidence
• freedom to fail
• clarity about my goal
• co-workers' support
• knowledge
• emotional support
• money
• the "return" looked worth it
• naïveté
• trust
• control of the situation
• freedom to make the decision and modify mistakes along the way

Circle the three "risk enablers" that are highest on your list in terms of being most necessary for you to be able to take a risk.

Is there a pattern, or is every case different?

Were most of your risks at a certain time in your life, or is there a wide range?

(For example, if your last risk was over 10 years ago, you just might be ready to take another one!)

PROFILE: CARL HIEBERT

*In 1986 Carl achieved an aviation first when he
flew an ultralight plane across Canada, to the
World Exposition in Vancouver, in a 5,000 mile,
58 day odyssey. Carl is a paraplegic due to a
hang-gliding accident in 1981. He is 44, an
ultralight flying instructor and a public speaker.*

THE RISK It would seem that the big risk was to take the
ultralight plane across Canada, a feat never done
before. In fact, the two years spent before that
date, trying to make it all happen, were more
difficult than the actual flight.

The biggest risks for me were at age 26, when I
bought my first house, began a serious
relationship, took up sky-diving and left the
Mennonite Church.

THE FEAR To stop being a part of the Mennonite Church
was an upheaval of my entire identity. It was
comparable to jumping out of an airplane at
5,000 feet. It affected me physically, emotionally
and spiritually. The Mennonite community is a
very close-knit one. If I wasn't part of it, who
was I?

THE RESULT I began a remarkable process of self-discovery.
The inner journey of religious freedom led me to
a greater awareness of myself and more tolerance
of others.

**"FEAR IS PART OF ANY RISK-TAKING AGENDA. NEVER
LOOK BACK AND SAY, "I WISH I WOULD HAVE" WHEN
IN FACT YOU PROBABLY HAD THE CHANCE."**

Age and Risk-taking

Age has little to do with risk-taking. Some young people find physical risk-taking easier, ("I'm twenty, and I'm invincible"), but some "older folks" get their pilot's license when they retire!

Peter Drucker, the respected management consultant, didn't write his first novel until he was 72 years old. When asked why, he said that he felt the novel was the supreme test of a writer and he didn't dare to make a fool of himself until *after* he was 70!

Many people find it easier to risk the older they get. It's all in the attitudes!

Risk Inhibitors

Often when we *don't* take risks there are valid reasons, such as:

- It didn't look worth it

- It didn't look like it would turn out

- The timing was all wrong

It *can* be a good decision to *not* risk. My concern, however, is when it looks like the risk could work out, the vision is a clear one and all systems say "go" but you *consistently* stop yourself, due to fear or a lack of courage. In this case, there may be a feeling of sadness, sorrow or failure for not risking. Do *not* blame yourself. If you *could* have risked, you *would* have. Look for patterns that you might want to change now.

Risk Inhibitors

List 3 risks you *wish* you had taken, but did not take.

Risks *Not* Taken

Personal	Occupational	Reason	Age

Risk Inhibitors

Q: When you decided to *not* take a risk, what stopped you?

A: Some common responses of participants:

- it made sense *not* to take the risk
- low self-confidence
- lack of qualifications
- too many qualifications
- family considerations
- dependents
- fear of being alone
- negative influences
- professional influences
- loss of financial security
- no financial resources
- fear of self-knowledge
- fear of looking foolish
- fear of being disliked
- fear of hurting others
- lack of momentum

Risk Inhibitors

One of the most common risk inhibitors is **FEAR**.
F E A R is an acronym for:

False
Evidence
Appearing
Real

In other words, we make it real by giving "the unknown" an energy and a belief. It might not even be a true belief.

For example, you're walking alone on a dark street at night. You hear a car following slowly behind you. No one is around. You turn the corner. So does the car. You turn to look and see one very large man in the car. He looks menacing. You walk faster. The car follows you at a faster rate. You slow down; so does the car. You hear the car stop, the door open and slam shut. You run. You hear footsteps running behind you.

At this point, adrenalin is probably pumping through your body. Your heart's throbbing; your throat's dry.

You turn the corner. He does not. He's *not* following you. You are safe.

You take 15 minutes to calm down. Nothing happened! But the fear was *real*. Your body could not tell the difference.

Our perception makes a situation real in our mind, whether it is real or not. Let's explore.

Fear and Doubt

FEAR: Anticipation of misfortune or pain

DOUBT: An unsettled state of opinion, a matter of uncertainty

FEAR	*DOUBT*
Negative	Positive
Incapacitating	"Capacitating"
Incapable of making plans	Capable of improving plans
Hooks into your gut	Temporarily shadows your strength
Makes you want to not go ahead	Makes you plan more carefully

It is natural to have fears and doubts. Release the fear. Use the doubt to improve your performance, and prepare for all the things that could go wrong.

PLAN, PREPARE, PLAN, PREPARE.

We will explore this in more detail in the "action" section further on in this guide.

Stress

It's true that risk-taking can raise your stress level. But that's how you know you're really alive. It's a positive reaction in many ways. There's a thrill, a rush, an excitement to risk-taking that makes it all fun, exciting and vibrant.

What if your stress level gets too high?
How do you handle it now?

❏ Eat more food	❏ Exercise (reasonably)
❏ Smoke	❏ Walk the dog (or yourself)
❏ Go to parties	❏ Listen to music
❏ Sleep all weekend	❏ Soak in a hot bath
❏ Buy donuts	❏ Get a good night's sleep
❏ Gorge on chocolate	❏ Visit a friend
❏ Exercise like a mad fiend	❏ Take some yoga classes
❏ Make lots and lots of plans in order to keep busier than a buzzing bee	❏ Write the problems down
	❏ Go to a movie
❏ Go shopping until you're ready to drop	❏ Drive through the country
❏ Get drunk	❏ Take a holiday
❏ Get sick	❏ Breathe slowly and deeply

Obviously, the list on the right is more positive and much better for you. Find healthy stress releasers that work and do them!

PROFILE: JONATHAN NELSON

Children are constantly taking risks as they grow. Jonathan is a tall, skinny, perceptive and funny eight-year old.

THE RISK   When I was seven years old and in grade two, I joined my school's swim team. There were forty-two kids, ages seven to eleven, and the practices were for forty-five minutes, three times a week.
I was one of the three youngest kids. After a few weeks, some kids made fun of me and I wanted to quit.

THE FEAR   Most of the kids were older and bigger than me. I felt afraid that I was the worst. I thought they would think that I wasn't any good.

THE RESULT   My coaches, Adriana and Bob, helped me a lot. I placed at the swim meet. I was faster than some kids. I got a ribbon, a sweatshirt and a really cool swim team jacket with a logo on it.

"DON'T LISTEN TO WHAT ANYONE ELSE SAYS. TRY NOT TO BE AFRAID. FEEL GOOD ABOUT YOURSELF AND TRY YOUR BEST."

OBJECTIVE 4:

Myths of Risk-Taking:

1. All risks are worth taking.

2. There is no right time to risk. You can take a risk anytime.

3. You should just "jump in" whenever you risk.

4. You don't need a fall-back plan.

5. Risk-takers aren't afraid to risk.

6. Entrepreneurs take lots of risks.

7. It's best if the risk is imposed on you.

NOT TRUE!

Facts

1. *All risks are worth taking.*

   You'd be mighty foolish to take some risks. If it doesn't look good to you, don't do it.

2. *There is no right time to risk. You can take a risk anytime.*

   There are right times to risk. For personal risk, it's best to be feeling strong, mentally and physically healthy and absolutely fired up by the vision of what you want. On a corporate level you must have the support or at the very least a very under-standing boss and co-worker.

3. *You should just "jump in" whenever you risk.*

Never! Use the risk cycle on page 60. All risks must be well planned. Once the plans are in place, there is the moment of truth when you do have to take the plunge.

4. *You don't need a fall-back plan.*

You always need at least one, if not six or seven, fall-back plans.

5. *Risk-takers aren't afraid to risk.*

Oh yes they are! Every risk-taker knows the accom-panying fear. The difference is that they will go ahead anyway. Fear does not stop them, it just makes them prepare more thoroughly.

6. *Entrepreneurs take lots of risks.*

Entrepreneurs obviously take risks, but they don't take a lot of them, willy-nilly. They know ways in which to minimize the risk to maximize the return.

7. *It's best if the risk is imposed on you.*

It's best to choose your risks wisely. There are two kinds of risk:

a) **Imposed risk,** such as an accident, death of a spouse, being fired. These situations often get the recipient moving into new ventures, but it's obvi-ously not the best way, and certainly not the easiest. People do, however, tend to carry on and manage quite well after the initial shock.

b) **Chosen risk.** It's always best to decide what you want to risk for, and when.

Risk-taking is a process that includes a number of stages. It is useful to use a *risk cycle,* as shown on the next page.

RISK CYCLE

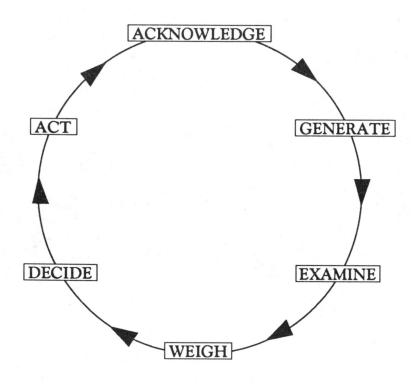

RISK CYCLE

1. **ACKNOWLEDGE** the situation as it exists now. It could be a positive situation, but you may feel that there must be something more, or that you can contribute in a different way or that it's time to move on to face new challenges and grow.

2. **GENERATE** options. This is the part that requires the courage to be creative and stcp out of the usual mold. Talk to people, read all the books you can find on a topic. Don't limit yourself in any way. Often we tend to see things as "either...or", or "black or white" when many more possibilities exist.

3. **EXAMINE** the options. Talk to several people. Work through some plans. Get support. Enlist people who can share your vision.

4. **WEIGH** the options. Use a decision-making tool, such as a decision analysis worksheet. Do a situational analysis, giving each option a score. These tools can be found in management texts on decision-making.

5. **DECIDE** what you are going to do. Is this a risk worth taking?

6. **ACT** as if there's no other way to do it. In the final moment, you must commit yourself to action and take a grand "leap of faith". What's required is a trust of yourself and the universe, in a sense. When you've done all you can, you need a sort of "spiritual fearlessness" to just DO IT...RISK!

PROFILE: BONNIE BICKEL

A former speech therapist and dress designer, Bonnie Bickel is, at 46, a wife, mother, entrepreneur and investor. As the originator of BB Bargoon's fabric and wallpaper discount stores, she is one of Canada's most successful businesswomen.

THE RISK When I started out selling clothing at home parties, in 1975, I had no money. The fashion party business was fairly successful, but after six years I wasn't having fun with it anymore. When I was renovating a house, I became frustrated by the tawdriness of bargain wallpaper shops and decided to open BB Bargoon's in 1981, to offer something better. No one thought it could fly, not my husband, accountant or lawyer. We put up our house as collateral to get the money to open.

THE FEAR When we decided to open a second, bigger store, it took our last dime. At 6:a.m. on the day of its opening I was so filled with fear, I had a migraine and couldn't move until noon. I was really afraid of falling flat on my face.

When I went into the store, I was so relieved to see customers, I burst into tears!

My other fear concerned my family. I was working really hard when many mothers were still at home with their children full-time. I had a nanny and a supportive husband, but I wondered if our girls would turn out all right.

THE RESULT I felt tremendous exhilaration from the success of the second store. Growing the business has been the fun part. We now have fourteen corporate stores and six franchises. We went from $60,000. to $14 million in nine years.

Our teenage daughters are doing really well.

"I DON'T EVER WANT TO SAY, 'IF ONLY...'"

There are now two "next steps"

1.   Think of a risk you did *not* take. Where did you stop on the risk cycle? Do you think you made a good decision? Think about some other risks you did not take. Do you tend to stop yourself in the same place on the cycle each time?

2.   Think of a risk you would like to take. At what stage of the risk cycle are you? Use the risk cycle to see *how* you can move into action.

Working The Risk Through: Disaster Plan

Once you know a risk you want to take, the fear of the unknown can creep in to get you. The best way to move into action is to "write it down". Prepare a disaster plan. Often the worst we can imagine becomes something very manageable once we write it down and look at it. Answer the questions below.

1. The Risk I would like to take

2. The Fears I have About This Risk
   a) What could happen (loss of job, status, other)
   b) How I might feel (embarrassed, foolish, wrong)
   c) What if I fail?

3. The Worst That Could Happen

4. What Could I Do If #3 Happened?

Expect the unexpected
Make clear contingency plans

5.   What Else Could I Do?

6.   Who Could Help Me? Who Else?

7.   What Are The Possible Gains?

8.   Is It Worth The Risk?

9.   What Will It Cost Me Not To Take This Risk?

10. Does This Idea Keep Coming To Me? What Does My Intuition Say?

How to Take Risks Wisely

Now you have a good working definition of risk-taking and you know just what it is; you know about personal and corporate attitudes toward risk-taking, the factors which enable and inhibit you from taking risks; you know how to use the risk cycle to analyze the risks you want to take and how to change fear into doubt.

Phew! So now what?

Well, I think we still need to know more about what's worth risking for. In other words...

What Gets You Hot?

PASSION.

Here's a fun page.

List all the things (I hope it's more than one!) that get you hot and "turn you on" —not what gets you hot under the collar and makes you angry, but what gets you excited? What puts a smile on your face and makes you feel good? What do you enjoy?

I've listed some of mine. Check the ones that are the same for you, then continue on to list at least 10 more of your own:

- ice cream in a pastry with hot fudge sauce on top

- warm sunny days when the birds are singing and the air smells sweet

- bittersweet dark chocolate

- cappucino with frothy milk

- moonlight shining on fresh snow

- bittersweet dark chocolate

- spring when the first daffodils and tulips poke out

- long walks through the woods

- my little boy's exuberance

- the oceanside

- bittersweet dark chocolate

- funny postcards from friends

- sex

- flowers

- lying in the sun at the beach
- taking a risk and having it work out well (of course!)
- bittersweet dark chocolate (always!)

Your list:

_____

_____

_____

_____

_____

_____

_____

_____

_____

_____

_____

_____

_____

_____

_____

_____

_____

_____

To Do

1. Share this question with some friends. Talk about what gets you hot. Then make some observations:

    A. Did you enjoy listing your "turn on" items?

    B. Did you find that you were starting to smile and feel good?

    C. When you share this question with friends and/or colleagues, did you notice an increase of energy?

When people discuss what "gets them hot", what they feel passionate about, energy is generated. This also happens with risk-taking.

Remember how it feels to fall in love? Suddenly you can survive on 4 hours of sleep and feel terrific.

That kind of excitement is also generated by taking risks. The energy is enough to make your toes dance across the sidewalk, to lead you to sing in the rain and ponder Paris in the springtime. Gene Kelly move over!

However, all risks need to be taken for something that you feel passionate about and have a vision for. It's critical to:

1. Have a strong sense of self.

2. Take your own risks, for your own vision.

3. Show courage, a spiritual fearlessness, and a trust in the universe.

How do we do this? First we need to understand what passion, confidence, courage, intuition, creativity and inspiration are. Then we need to overcome our fear of these qualities and our own power.

When I talk about power, I mean it in a positive sense. When you are "Power-FULL", you are filled with your own sense of self, your talents, gifts and uniqueness which is your's to share with the world. You need to believe in yourself. You have the ability to make a difference to others in a positive way.

PASSION: Intense emotion, zeal and enthusiasm

Run down the street on a beautiful, sunny day, arms flung wide open, head back and mouth smiling, and shout, "What a fine, fine day!"

Can you do it? Children do this all the time. (Well, maybe not in those exact words!) It's really too bad when we have our passion dampened by what's proper and acceptable behavior, by what's adult, by the hurt and pain we absorb in our growing up that tempers our enthusiasm for anything. We need to allow ourselves to feel passionately; we need to have fun!

RISK-TAKING INVOLVES THE ABILITY TO FEEL PASSIONATELY ABOUT SOMETHING IN ORDER TO MAKE IT HAPPEN.

In grade eleven, a teacher gave me a copy of the book, *The Agony and the Ecstasy*. It is about the life of Michaelangelo. I knew basically nothing about art, but I became totally engrossed in the artist's ability to carve the marble into the statue of the David. I decided then and there that when I finished university, I was going to Italy to see Michaelangelo's sculpture. No one believed I would do it; my friends laughed and said, "You're not a traveller." I left by ship from New York in September 1969, bound for Europe, and Italy in particular, for one year. That year changed my life. It was the passion of Irving Stone writing about the passion of Michaelangelo that inspired me.

Taking the risk of hitch-hiking through Europe, first with a girlfriend, and then alone, with only a knapsack and very little money, took all the courage I could muster. It also increased my self-confidence, allowed me to come to know my instincts, and trust my intuition. Travelling opened my eyes and my heart to life more than I would ever have thought possible.

PROFILE: JOHN KIM BELL

JOHN KIM BELL, age 38, is a Native Canadian from the Mohawk Nation, a musical conductor, composer, producer, impressario, lobbyist and activist. He is the founder and President of the Canadian Native Arts Foundation which exposes native children to arts performances and gives arts scholarships.

THE RISK Creating the Native Arts Foundation in 1986 was a risk. I had skills as a pianist but no political clout or particular knowledge to become a businessman and lobbyist. I had to somehow counter all the people who said you're a nice young man but you won't be able to do this.

THE FEAR I was afraid that I'd make a total fool of myself. Even though I took out a personal loan of one-quarter of a million dollars, it wasn't the money that bothered me, but whether or not I had "the right stuff".
My Self, my own identity, was on the line.

THE RESULT I decided I would make the Native Arts Council a success although it tested every fibre of my being to develop the projects, especially the concert and Native ballet. We provided a forum for all those who were unsure of what being an Indian means. This was their chance to counter the great suppression of our Native language and culture.
It was a process of self-discovery in front of the public.

"YOU MUST PUT THE MOST PERSONAL PART OF YOUR-SELF ON THE LINE TO ACHIEVE ANYTHING. LIFE IS SHORT. DON'T LET FEAR STOP YOU."

Courage

Walter Anderson, an author, calls courage a three letter word, "YES".

Often we think we can't do something, or believe we're not talented enough, or smart enough or "anything" enough. We are our own harshest judges; waiting to be "whatever" enough, never trying anything. If we sincerely want to do it, all we have to do is say "yes" to it.

Often the commitment alone will bring about the support that's needed. People get excited by our enthusiasm and vision of what we want to make happen. It might be easier than you think to get the support you need. Or it could be difficult and take a long, long time.

One thing is certain. Nothing will happen unless you respond to your intuition, show courage and say "yes" to your idea.

How do you get confident enough to believe you can do it? By saying "yes" and doing it. Take the risk in spite of your fears.

PROFILE: MARG GLEESON

Marg Gleeson, at age 49, is a speaker, lecturer and advisor to the police in dealing with domestic violence. She was an abused child and wife.

THE RISK In 1969, during one of his violent rages, my husband broke my neck. I had to decide whether or not to have neck surgery, in a new procedure for that time. There was only a 50% chance of living, and beyond that, a 50% chance of being paralyzed or not.

THE FEAR I feared that I wouldn't be there for my four young children, more than I did for my life. The doctors told me that even if I lived, I wouldn't be able to hold my baby. At the time I was 27 years old, 5'7", and weighed only 90 lb. I thought, "I can't risk anything going wrong. I will be normal."

THE RESULT The operation worked. Five years later, I finally left my husband. My kids are doing well.

Just after my surgery, I had this out-of-body experience. I knew I had to live for some special purpose. In my forties, I began to work toward the treatment of the whole family, and to promote the intense treatment of male abusers immediately.

I want to do everything I can so that no one will ever go through what I went through.

"WHEN WE TAKE RISKS WE LEARN MORE ABOUT LIFE. WITH EACH MISTAKE WE ARE GIVEN THE OPPORTUNITY TO GET A NEW LESSON."

Confidence

Often people will say to me, "That's fine for you to take risks, but I'm not very confident." Confidence is boldness, a firm trust and an assured state of mind. Believe me, I was never confident. I still agonize over each and every risk that I take. I was raised in a sea of negativity. You know how some kids are born with a silver spoon in their mouth? Well, I was born with a band-aid, just in case!

You take risks so you can learn about yourself. When you accomplish your goal, your confidence gets boosted. It's a positive, upward spiral.

We have to take risks in order to go beyond our usual, self-imposed limitations. There simply is no other way to learn about yourself than to embrace life and its challenges—even if it means creating those challenges. You must make it happen. If you feel that destiny is in your own hands, that you have a say in your life, then you will seek opportunities for growth.

How do you know what's worth risking for? Your intuition will tell you, if you'll listen.

PROFILE: BONNEY KING

Bonney is the single mom of two teenagers. She has been on her own for seven years with basically no financial or family support. She is a former teacher with B.A.and B.Ed. degrees.

THE RISK I had a good job with a workshop company hiring instructors, shaping the programs and writing promotional copy, but after a few years I was bored. I knew I wanted to get into advertising. Although I had to support my children, I decided to accept a job as a copywriter even though it paid only half the income.

THE FEAR I was afraid that I couldn't support my family on such little money.

I had a fear of failing miserably, that I'd be no good or worse still, that after making all these changes, I wouldn't like it.

THE RESULT After one and a half years, I was offered a job at higher pay with another company. When I went to resign, my boss asked me to stay, matched the "new" salary and gave me a car allowance. So in effect, I regained my former, higher income, plus another $13,000 a year and benefits. And I was doing what I wanted to do.

"TAKING RISKS BECOMES EASIER AND YOUR SELF-CONFIDENCE BUILDS WITH EACH STEP YOU TAKE."

*TO COMPREHEND THE RELATIONSHIP OF INTUITION,
CREATIVITY AND RISK-TAKING TO INNOVATION*

Intuition

Intuition is instinctive knowledge. We know something
without really knowing how we know. For some people
it's accompanied by a physical sensation, hence "gut
feeling", an actual sense of a grabbing in the stomach.
When I ask seminar participants if they have experienced
intuition, over 75% of them say yes, and an even greater
percent recognize a physical sensation of some kind.
Some get a tenseness, a feeling of excitement, an
aliveness in their muscles. I get shivers on the back of my
neck when something is intuitively right.

An energy accompanies intuition. People feel more
in-tune, alive, excited. Often the thought or dream or
hunch just won't quit. It's like a little nagging puppy
tugging on your pant leg to play.

It's important to be in a state of readiness, to hear
your intuition speak and to listen to it when it does.

Intuitive Readiness

Allow some quiet time in your life. Unplug the walkman,
get off the phone, turn off the TV, go for a walk. Sit
quietly and stare at a candle flame. Soak in a hot tub.
You can't hear your inner voice unless you listen to it.

Intuition and Risk

Your intuition tells you what's worth risking for. It's a crime to ignore it. It's different than wishful thinking, grandiose, ego-generated, get-rich-quick-schemes and unhealthy intent.

Intuition is your inner voice, God, higher consciousness, spirit guide or life force trying to inspire you to fulfill your destiny. I believe it is our job on earth to discover our particular gift or talent, and then use it to make the world better in some way.

Creativity

To create is to originate in some way, to discover a connection between seemingly unrelated thoughts, objects or patterns.

Woodrow Wilson said creativity was looking at the world through a fresh pair of eyes.

I used to think that I wasn't creative, that to be creative I had to be in the studio, paintbrush in hand, working on a mural of gigantic proportions to rave reviews. Nonsense.

We can be creative in so many different ways—in developing new methods of hiring personnel, in dealing with a child's tantrum, in scheduling gym times for workouts, in corporate re-shufflings, in priority setting, in eliminating toxic wastes, in creating work programs for the unemployed.

Creative is not something you become, it's not something to grab onto or reach for which is external to you. Creativity is within all of us; it's something to release and rejoice in.

How do you do it? Ya gotta shake up your bones a little. DO SOMETHING DIFFERENT !!!!!!!!

Ways To Release Your Creativity

What would be a change for you?

1. Laugh
2. Tell jokes
3. Soak in a tub by candlelight
4. Go for a walk
5. Listen to music, especially classical
6. See a foreign movie
7. See a play
8. Go to a baseball game
9. Go to the ballet
10. Read funny cards in a store
11. Buy funny cards and send yourself one each week
12. Eat out at a Japanese restaurant
13. If you're Japanese, go to a Deli
14. Take a course in something totally different for you
15. Change your route for going to work
16. Take a day off work to read mysteries
17. Bake a cake
18. Go to the zoo
19. Go on a holiday to somewhere really different
20. Spend 4 hours in total silence

What else could you do?

1. _____
2. _____
3. _____
4. _____
5. _____

Creativity and Risk

In order to break the "either...or" syndrome, we need to generate many, many options for the "both...and" solution. Once we know what we want, what our vision is, creativity is needed to find ways to make the vision happen.

Intuition, Creativity, Risk-Taking and Innovation

To innovate is to create a new way of doing something that will improve the existing way. It is not the act of changing things just for change's sake. There is some truth to the expression, "If it ain't broke, don't fix it." The problem is that the person who has a fresh idea is alone at first and may have trouble showing others that the idea is a good one. For that reason, the person who innovates must be a risk-taker.

The innovator starts with an intuitive idea, some "flash", and "aha" experience. He or she then has to take the risk of putting the idea forward.

Dare to Dream

Creativity is needed to come up with solutions to the problems, discomfort and probable disbelief toward the idea. In an organization, some political savvy is needed as well.

The innovator needs to state the vision clearly, to get the team together and go for it. The company has to provide the receptivity for the innovation. You need to convince, influence and build partnerships for success.

PROFILE: JOHN EASTON

Formerly in the sports car business and a pub owner in England, John Easton moved to Canada in 1965. He is an Ontario-based real-estate developer and owner of several companies who, at age 47, is also involved in spiritual growth through yoga, massage and t'ai chi.

THE RISK In Canada I became very successful in developing real estate transactions for other people. In 1985 I saw I could do it for myself and became involved in projects in excess of $70 million. I was never afraid of failure or losing the money, because I would still have my family and health. The big risk for me was the probable loss of freedom.

THE FEAR For years I was used to being a free spirit, sailing and wandering on the beaches in other countries and living in my house in Spain for months at a time.

I was very apprehensive about how bound I would be once I made the commitment to run my own real estate development company.

THE RESULT Although money was never the motive, I did become financially successful. It's been rewarding to take old buildings and warehouses and convert them to appealing environments, such as the Ontario Design Centre and Dominion Square. I discovered my own creativity in the discussions of form, colour and style.

"ANYONE CAN GO ALONG IN A MUNDANE FASHION. WITHOUT CHANGE AND CHALLENGE YOU MIGHT AS WELL BE DEAD."

Objective 6:

TO LEARN HOW YOU AND YOUR COMPANY CAN BE
MUTUALLY SUPPORTIVE IN ORDER TO TAKE THE RISKS
NECESSARY TO INNOVATE

After the Peters and Waterman book, *In Search of Excellence*, was published, some managers walked among their staff saying, "We have to get excellent around here." Of course, most people had no idea of what they were talking about, let alone how to go about it.

I would hate the same thing to happen with innovation.

There has to be a reason to innovate, first and foremost.

No one should innovate because it's the new buzz word, the new "in" thing to do.

First there needs to be a vision.

Vision

Your vision is your dream, your intuitive answer to the questions, "What do I want?", "What would I like to see happen?" If it is linked to your life purpose (if you have any sense of that) then so much the better. For example, if your life purpose is to promote honesty between people, and you teach courses in clear communication or lead group therapy sessions, you are realizing your purpose. It's also quite all right for a vision to be very specific and practical. Your vision could be to get improved work conditions including a decent lunch room for the staff. It's important to work toward making your vision a reality, instead of the other way around, which is to give it up and forget about it—less risky, more safe, and certainly in line with the "don't rock the boat" lesson. How do you get support in order to break away from the C.Y.A.* corporate school of thought?

* cover your anatomy

GETTING SUPPORT

Individual Support

1. Have a clear sense of vision, know what you want to accomplish and why.

2. Act confident.

3. Find the people who will understand your vision and work with you.

4. Prepare, prepare, prepare. Research well.

5. Take small risks in other areas to build up your risk tolerance and your self-confidence.

6. Understand what risk is, that the fear is normal and that you must display courage.

7. Know that you may have to put your job on the line. Have more than one back-up plan.

8. Enlist the emotional support of family and friends.

9. Find other risk-takers. Ask them questions. Get answers. Avoid negative people.

10. Be in top mental, physical and emotional condition. You'll need stamina, faith, and a spiritual fearlessness to see you through.

Corporate Support

1. Commit time, money and personnel to new projects. In other words, put your money where your mouth is. No one will risk for a few token words.

2. Give "change" time. Don't announce and impose changes quickly.

3. Allow open communication. Keep people informed.

4. If you can't risk "upwards", risk "downwards". Teach managers how to be open to new ideas from others.

5. Set up a reward system. If money is impossible, make it time, status, freedom to choose new projects, ways to have more input.

6. Don't dictate a vision. People will risk for a vision they share and have had some input to. Use negotiation skills.

7. Encourage people. Give them incentives and opportunities to take seminars, learn and grow. Nurture your staff.

8. Trust your people. Treat them like adults, not children.

9. Allow mistakes. Admit them quickly and fix them right away.

10. Run outside interference for your staff. You look after the politics, let them look after making the ideas work.

Innovation

Innovation requires a trust in the future. It's a team approach that requires an individual to be the initiator, to take the risks and gather the forces of the corporation to make the vision a reality.

I believe it's absolutely essential for the organization to become proactive in order to meet today's challenging economy, changing society and individuals' rights.

It's the person who has vision, the ability to lead and take risks who will be in the forefront of innovation and change.

Organization

Past-directed	*Future Oriented*
Reactive	Proactive
Incapacitated by fear	Moving in spite of fear
Stagnated	Innovative
Afraid to risk	Willing to risk

The priest who was with Senator Jacques Hébert when he went on the hunger strike in the Canadian Parliament Buildings to save the Katimavik Youth Program said,

"We seek to live on a higher plane, to become something greater than we are, to build a better world. And we know that a change of structures without a change of heart will not make the situation any better."

The time has come for the organization to recognize the individual within. The time has come to allow some heart into the organization, to lead with passion, compassion and courage. It is now time to take the risks for a better world.

PROFILE: FRED RYAN

From the age 17 to now, at 70, Fred Ryan has, on average, changed careers every five years. He's been a butcher, a painter, a cook for 17,000 in a survey crew in northern British Columbia, a photographer, a camera shop-owner, a walkie-talkie importer, a real estate salesperson, an audio-visual equipment supplier, a shopping centre manager, an events manager and finally, a manufacturer.

THE RISK   Changing jobs is my way of life. I depend on my wife, companions and employees. When one of my businesses is going well, I get bored. I sell it and start something else.

THE FEAR   I don't feel much stress or fear. Maybe some apprehension. I never lose sleep.

THE RESULT Some businesses do better than others. I have little concern for monetary things. My family and pals matter the most. This is my way of life.

"TOO MANY PEOPLE FEAR BEING LET GO BY THEIR COMPANIES. DON'T EXPECT FAVOURS. DO SOMETHING YOU ENJOY AND HAVE CONFIDENCE IN YOUR OWN TALENTS."

Innovation – "Off The Top of Your Head" Answers

Read the following questions. Jot down the first response that "pops" into your head. Use just a few words. It's important to answer quickly before you have a chance to "judge" your response.

A. How can you affect the...

    (a) circumstances
    (b) environment
    (c) level of encouragement in your organization in order to innovate?

a)   *circumstances:* _____

     _____

     _____

     _____

b)   *environment:* _____

     _____

     _____

     _____

c)   *encouragement:* _____

     _____

     _____

     _____

B. Consider the...

    (a) Generation of changes, the individuals involved and their ideas

    (b) The acceptance of the innovation—is there a team?

    (c) The implementation—is there trust and team collaboration?

What can you do?

_____

_____

_____

_____

What are the perceived risks?

_____

_____

_____

_____

C. Action Plan

a) What will you do?

_____

_____

_____

_____

b) What do you expect from others?

_____

_____

_____

_____

c) What do you expect from yourself?

_____

_____

_____

_____

Innovation and Vision

This is how "VISION" relates to "GOALS" and "TASKS"

Vision: The vision is broad, it answers the question, "What do I want?"

Goals: The goals are specific, measurable and attainable.

Tasks: The tasks are very specific and are given a date for completion

Example:
Vision

The new people we hire fit in well with the organization. They are a productive asset to our group. They feel useful and free to contribute their ideas. Morale is good and there is very little staff turnover.

Goals:
(support the vision)

1.   Generate ten new, innovative hiring procedures that we can examine as a group.

2.   Poll staff to discover feelings now present about existing hiring procedures.

3.   Find out about companies which have hired people through the front lines workers instead of senior staff. Has it worked out?

Tasks: (specific and date-set)	Date Due	Date Completed
1. Set up meeting with Brian and Jo-Anne this Thursday.		
2. Phone 3 companies to discuss their new hiring procedures.		
3. Develop questionnaire. Call in Betty and Rod.		
4. Get Human Resources people to lunch meeting to brainstorm and update.		
5. View new hiring video.		

Innovation Worksheet

You can do this exercise more than once. Choose whether you want to work on a personal or organizational vision.

1. My vision for myself, the organization or division or department: (Answer the question, "What do I want"?)

    _____
    _____
    _____
    _____
    _____
    _____
    _____

2. My goals:

    _____
    _____
    _____
    _____
    _____
    _____
    _____

3. Specific Tasks: Due Date   Completed

a)		
b)		
c)		
d)		
e)		

4. The Risks:

_____
_____
_____
_____
_____
_____
_____

5. My Fears:

_____
_____
_____
_____
_____
_____
_____

6. Objectives:

    a) _____

    _____

    b) _____

    _____

    c) _____

    _____

7. I can get support in these ways:

    a) _____

    _____

    b) _____

    _____

    c) _____

    _____

8. What it will cost me not to attempt to make this vision a reality:

    _____

    _____

    _____

    _____

    _____

    _____

    _____

9. What I can gain:

_____

_____

_____

_____

_____

_____

_____

_____

10. My vision, stated as a definite accomplishment that has happened:

_____

_____

_____

_____

_____

_____

_____

PROFILE: JUNE CALLWOOD

Author of twenty-four books, writer of numerous magazine articles, newspaper columnist, television host, and one of the strongest activists and voices for social justice in Canada, June Callwood has taken on several controversial causes. She established such centres as Jessie's for teenagers, Nellie's Hostel for Women and Casey House Hospice for AIDS patients. She has received numerous honours and awards.

THE RISK Sometimes I lose friends because of my beliefs. Two of the most difficult stands I've taken have been pro-choice, because of the abuse from pro-life groups, and anti-censorship of any kind. I have to speak my mind, as do my friends. We cannot do differently.

THE FEAR There's not much fear in me; I come from a very secure background of French, Indian and Loyalist. It's harder for others to be open or conspicuous, I think. They're the truly brave ones.

I have a strong marriage and supportive adult children. It's like sitting on a rock. My only fear is of my family being hurt. I would never jeopardize their feelings.

THE RESULT As a writer I was able to meet people and get first-hand information. I knew when I was right and society was wrong. Now organizations exist that caused so much upset at the time. After a few years people forget it was ever an issue.

Each person deserves to be able to stand up with some dignity.

"BECOMING IMMOBILIZED DUE TO A FEAR OF LOOKING FOOLISH CAN MAKE YOU ILL. BY DOING SOMETHING TO FIGHT INJUSTICE YOU WILL HAVE LIVED A HEALTHIER, USEFUL LIFE."

Summary: **RISK** *it!*

1. Keep focused on your vision and the results that you want.

2. Act, don't react. Don't risk because of an emotional response such as anger.

3. Take your own risks, not anyone else's.

4. Be committed to your risk and get the support you need.

5. Put in 100% effort. Risk is not tentative.

6. There are no guarantees.

7. Anticipate and prepare for potential problems. Stay flexible.

8. Recognize your fear. Know it is natural and risk anyway.

9. Know that with any risk and change there is loss.

10. Visualize your success. Be ready to accept it.

Inspiration

Many people have commented on risk-taking, vision and living fully. Circle three quotes that inspire you the most. Write them out and put them in a prominent place where you will read them each day.

Security is mostly a superstition...Life is either a daring adventure or nothing.

— Helen Keller,
Author

Nothing great was ever achieved without enthusiasm. We are always getting ready to live but never living.

— Ralph Waldo Emerson,
Philosopher

Whatever you invest in, always keep one final rule in mind: take risks, but don't let them take you.

— Max Gunther,
Financial Analyst

A good businessman always decides to risk on his own judgment.

— David Viscott,
Author

Somewhere behind every risk should be a life worth risking for.

— David Viscott,
Author

I failed my way to success.

> — Thomas Edison,
> *Inventor*

Dream lofty dreams, and as you dream, so shall you become. Your vision is the promise of what you shall one day be.

> — James Allen,
> *Philosopher*

To be a success you need drive, determination, a belief in yourself and the willingness to take risks.

> — George Cohon,
> *President,*
> *McDonald's Canada*

We make a living by what we get. We make a life by what we give.

> — Unknown

Forming a vision calls on the capacity to take risks, to suffer change, to give up the present for a limbo state between what is and what will be.

> — E.G. Collins,
> *Former Editor,*
> *Harvard Business Review*

Any successful person has chosen action against inaction. In any initiative or opportunity pursuit there is an element of risk.

> — Edward deBono,
> *Author*

Risk-taking Reminders

- Everyone makes mistakes.

- We learn from our mistakes.

- It takes energy to stay in one place and not take risks.

- We probably have more to gain than we have to lose.

- Each risk is an attempt to achieve something worthwhile.

- We're either living fully or we're just existing.

Thought:

What would it say on your tombstone if you died this second?

Exercise:

Write what you would like inscribed on your tombstone. How would you like to be remembered?

_____

_____

_____

_____

_____

_____

_____

_____

Steps:

What action will you take *now* to start you on your way?

_____

_____

_____

_____

_____

_____

_____

_____

The misconception is that life happens to us. It doesn't. We happen to it. Be 100% committed to what you do. Take the responsibility. Otherwise all we're doing by living is not dying.

EMBRACE LIFE. TAKE THE RISK.

> **"TO KNOW AND TRUST ONE'S OWN TRUTH IS THE GREATEST RISK AND THE MOST ESSENTIAL RISK OF ALL."**
>
> — Reva Nelson

Suggested Reading:

Anderson, Walter, *Courage is a Three-Letter Word*, Ballantine, N.Y., 1986

Buscaglia, Leo, *Living, Loving & Learning*, Ballantine, N.Y., 1982.

Covey, Stephen, *The Seven Habits of Highly Effective People*, Simon & Schuster, N.Y., 1989

DeBono, Edward, *Tactics*, Little, Brown & Co., London, 1984

Drucker, Peter, *The Effective Executive*, Harper & Row, N.Y., 1983

Ferguson, Marilyn, *The Aquarian Conspiracy*, Tarcher, Calif., 1980

Freedman, Martha, *Overcoming the Fear of Success*, Seaview, N.Y., 1981

Fritz, Robert, *The Path of Least Resistance*, DMA Inc, Mass., 1984

Gawain, Shakti, *Creative Visualization*, Whatever Publishing, Calif., 1979

Gawain, Shakti, *Living in the Light*, Whatever Publishing, Calif., 1986

Glasser, William, *Take Effective Control of Your Life*, Harper & Row, N.Y. 1984

Kanter, Rosabeth Moss, *The Change Masters*, Simon & Schuster, N.Y., 1983

Keyes, Ralph, *Chancing It*, Little, Brown & Co., Boston, 1985

Lerner, Harriet, *The Dance of Anger*, Harper & Row, N.Y., 1985

Lichenstein, Grace, *Machisma, Women & Daring*, Doubleday, N.Y., 1981

May, Rollo, *The Courage to Create*, Bantam, N.Y., 1976

NOTES

Suggested Reading (continued)

Miller, Donald, *Personal Vitality*, Addison Wesley, California, 1977

Morgan, Gareth, *Images of an Organization*, Sage, California, 1986

Naisbitt, John, *Megatrends*, Warner, N.Y., 1982

Peck, Scott, *The Road Less Travelled*, Simon & Schuster, N.Y., 1978

Peters, Tom, *Thriving on Chaos*, Alfred Knopf, N.Y., 1987

Potter, Beverly, *The Way of the Ronin*, Amacom, N.Y., 1984

Rowan, Roy, *The Intuitive Manager*, Little, Brown & Co., Boston, 1986

Rubin, Theodore Isaac, *Overcoming Indecisiveness*, Harper & Row, N.Y., 1985

Sinetar, Marsha, *Do What You Love, The Money Will Follow*, Dell, N.Y., 1987

Sher, Barbara, *Wishcraft*, Ballantine, N.Y., 1979

Siegelman, Ellen, *Personal Risk*, Harper & Row, N.Y., 1983

Simon, Sidney, *Getting Unstuck*, Warner, N.Y., 1988

Toffler, Alvin, *Future Shock*, Random House, N.Y., 1970

Trungpa, Chogyam, *Shambala*, Shambala Publications, Boston, 1984

Viorst, Judith, *Necessary Losses*, Ballantine, N.Y., 1986

Viscott, David, *Risking*, Simon & Schuster, N.Y., 1977

Wagner, Jane, *The Search for Signs of Intelligent Life in the Universe*, Wagner, N.Y., 1986

NOTES

ABOUT THE AUTHOR

REVA NELSON'S varied education and work experiences in Psychology, Education and Human Resources enable her to bring a special texture and richness to her seminars.

Since 1982, when she formed her own company, Reva has motivated organizations to communicate clearly, take risks and innovate. She is committed to inspiring individuals and businesses to take action for positive growth through her humourous and well-researched speeches.

A graduate of the University of Western Ontario, Reva is often sought out as the guest expert for radio, television and print interviews. She resides in Toronto with one son, one puppy, two cats and two fish.

MEETING PLANNERS

"Judging by the laughter, everyone thoroughly enjoyed your speech."

> — John Anderson,
> *Assistant V.P.*
> *Information Systems*
> *Planning*
> *Sun Life Assurance*
> *Company*

"The response to your session was terrific, as the attached glowing evaluations show."

> — Ingrid Norrish,
> *Director, Conferences*
> *and Seminar Services,*
> *Humber College*

REVA NELSON can help you be successful at your next event. Call, write or fax for information about these seminars and speeches:

- **SPEAK EASY: PANIC-FREE PRESENTATION SKILLS**

- **MEETINGS FOR RESULTS**

- **POSITIVE RISK-TAKING FOR POWERFUL RESULTS**

- **INTUITION AT WORK**

- **WHEN LAUGH LINES MEET LIFE LINES**

Words.Worth Professional Communications
58 Ellsworth Avenue, Ste. 347
Toronto, Ontario, Canada
M6G 2K3

Tel: (416) 656-0994
Fax: (416) 652-8536

RISK *it!*

by Reva Nelson

Couldn't someone you know benefit from reading *RISK it!*? It is the perfect gift for a colleague who's fearful of making a change, the executive wanting to inspire people to put forward fresh ideas or for a friend who's stuck in a rut.

Please send me _____ copies of *RISK it!*
I have enclosed a cheque made payable to
Words.Worth Professional Communications for $16.95 + $5.05 (tax, shipping and handling) each in the amount of _____ copies x $22.= $_____.

Full Name:_____
Address:_____
City:_____
Province (State):_____
Postal (Zip) Code:_____

Telephone: (   )_____

SEND ORDERS TO:

Words.Worth Professional Communications
58 Ellsworth Avenue, Ste. 347
Toronto, Ontario, Canada
M6G 2K3
Phone: (416) 656-0994 / Fax: (416) 652-8536

❑ Please send autographed copies
❑ Please inscribe the book(s) with this message:

_____
_____
_____

THERE IS A DISCOUNT
FOR LARGE ORDERS:
25 copies or more – 10%
100 copies or more – 20%
500 copies or more – 30%

(Please allow four to six weeks for delivery.)

RISK *it!*

by Reva Nelson

Couldn't someone you know benefit from reading *RISK it!*? It is the perfect gift for a colleague who's fearful of making a change, the executive wanting to inspire people to put forward fresh ideas or for a friend who's stuck in a rut.

Please send me _____ copies of *RISK it!*
I have enclosed a cheque made payable to **Words.Worth Professional Communications** for $16.95 + $5.05 (tax, shipping and handling) each in the amount of _____ copies x $22.= $_____.

Full Name:_____

Address:_____

City:_____

Province (State):_____

Postal (Zip) Code:_____

Telephone: (   )_____

SEND ORDERS TO:

Words.Worth Professional Communications
58 Ellsworth Avenue, Ste. 347
Toronto, Ontario, Canada
M6G 2K3
Phone: (416) 656-0994 / Fax: (416) 652-8536

❑ Please send autographed copies
❑ Please inscribe the book(s) with this message:

_____
_____
_____

> THERE IS A DISCOUNT
> FOR LARGE ORDERS:
> *25 copies or more – 10%*
> *100 copies or more – 20%*
> *500 copies or more – 30%*

(Please allow four to six weeks for delivery.)